From I to WE

The Round Table Journey

From I to WE

———————

The Round Table Journey

by

J. Zink

Jeffrey A. Zink

Thomas A. Kardashian

Peak Press
Colorado Springs

Peak Press
Printed in the United States of America
ISBN 1-892360-20-9
First Printing, December, 2004

"Catch 'Em Being Good"

Writing a book based on years of cumulative experience presents special challenges when it comes to thanking those who have supported the birthing process. So, at the risk of offending many of those whose love and support are hidden in the text, we limit our public gratitude to two groups:

First, we are deeply grateful to those friends and colleagues who took the time and meticulous effort to edit and proof our work: John Bedrosian, Joan Kardashian, Dr. Bill Nance, and Katharine Venema. With great enthusiasm, they answered our call for help and provided insightful suggestions that made this work richer and of deeper practical value.

Secondly, and critically important, we extend our heartfelt thanks to the nearly one thousand Round Table members who readily embraced the process, and thus provided the practical lens through which our hypothesis has been refined and ultimately proven viable. As we have helped them, they have surely helped us—and you.

Introduction

In recent years it has become apparent to those who study the debilitating factors of stress in the workplace that the stress levels of American executives have risen to such intolerable levels that keeping people healthy, motivated, and feeling that they are doing something worthwhile with their lives has become one of the major commercial challenges of the 21st Century.

There are many factors creating this situation. The more salient of these are well-known:

1. Increasing corporate competition in a world of limited resources;

2. Decreasing loyalty to the organization and loyalty to its employees;

3. Mergers, acquisitions and the resultant clash of corporate cultures;

4. The incessant intrusion of technology that forces people *to* work who are not *at* work;

5. The disconnect between one's work and one's spirituality that often results in depression;

6. The time and focus needs of the workplace that conflict with the demands of family and spousal relationships;

7. The rise of workaholism;

8. Sleep deprivation; and finally

9. The usual in-fighting, back-biting, politicking and general "healthy competition" as executives vie for the limited number of spaces "at the top."

This book makes no claim to completely resolve any or all of these issues in American business. But in recent years our team has developed a comprehensive and systemic strategy to reduce some of these issues to manageable levels. So we thought it sensible and prudent to share what we have done and exactly how we did it in order that you might benefit from our practices, improve upon them, and in general develop more effective strategies to help people.

This book will help you create an emotionally safe place in your culture for the authenticity that engenders trust and reduces stress. While addressing these difficult issues may improve the overall functionality of your organization and greatly please your stakeholders, our true purpose is to reduce your stress levels.

This is the mission of our lives: *Help People Heal.*

J. Zink, Ph.D.
Jeffrey Zink, Ph.D.
Tom Kardashian, Ph.D.

Los Angeles and Colorado Springs

Contents

Part I: Making It

ONE

The Round Table

Our wills and fates do so contrary run
That our devices still are overthrown;
Our thoughts are ours, their ends none of our own.

Hamlet, Act III, Scene II

The Round Table as an historical and literary image originates from Western Medieval literature in a body of work that scholars refer to as "Arthuriana." These are legends that writers down through the centuries used to create stories concerning a mythic or possibly real British king named Arthur. Quite possibly based on folk tales regarding a real Welsh king named "Artos The Bear," these stories inevitably included a seminal story of how King Arthur brought peace and prosperity to his divided and contentious kingdom by establishing a "Round Table" of his principal knights for the purpose of wise governance of his land.

When we were forming our interdisciplinary team to do the work we are doing with corporate executives, we naturally gravitated to the image of the Round Table because the original Round Table of King Arthur suggested that the knights who sat around it were all of equal value to the Round Table Journey. This, of course, is at odds with the typical structure of most corporations: A board of directors who oversees the actions and decisions of a Chief Executive Officer, who oversees the activities of a Chief Operating Officer, and so forth down the line, mirroring what classical philosophers called The Great Chain of Being, creating a large and cumbersome pyramid of power and control. Where one fits in the organizational chart often says something about his/her power, compensation, perquisites, opportunities for advancement, and other "pecking order" issues.

Such a structure, often referred to as "Command & Control," has been the principal model for business for a long time. Essentially a wartime model, it seems natural to structure a company in this manner, especially when business leaders often have seen themselves as warriors conducting great battles for limited resources and market share. It wasn't very long ago that one of the most popular business books was the 5th century BC Chinese General Sun Tzu's *The Art Of War*.

The Command & Control mindset issues marching orders "from the top," and "at the highest levels," and "straight from the corner office" that inevitably result in "I was just following orders" as a logical response when things go wrong. And things, of course, almost always go wrong. This fact alone creates the kind of stress that can paralyze an organization and do serious harm to the individuals in it. Let us not forget that people die in war.

So when we were asked to help create a mechanism for reducing the stress loads on high level executives and help them live healthier lives, our first task was to kill the metaphor of war itself.

Furthermore, we did not want to create more stress by declaring and waging war on stress; nor were we going to interview a bunch of executives, write an extensive and expensive report that says essentially, "Yep, it's bad alright," and hand our clients the bill.

We wanted to *be* the solution we were trying to create.

We wanted to *be* the solution we were seeking, so we knew that we had to be members of our own Round Tables—partners with our clients. Not just leaders, or consultants, or the gurus of the moment. We all had seen or had been the "program of the week," and knew that systemic behavior change just did not happen that way.

One of the three of us, Tom Kardashian, has been a member of the Young Presidents' Organization—YPO. Founded by a remarkable man named Ray Hickok in 1950, this publicly low-profile and exceptionally high-powered organization only accepts members who, at a minimum, have become President and Chief Executive Officer of a company with a minimum of 50 employees and annual revenues of more than $8 million by age forty-five. The mainstay purpose of the organization is "to create better leaders through Education and Idea Exchange." Along with bringing in outside "resources" to lecture and teach, the heart and soul of YPO is something called Forum. Simply put, Forum is a monthly meeting of no more than twelve members who meet for at least a half a day to discuss issues in every area of their lives. Conducted under the strictest confidentiality, these meetings provide opportunities for peers to talk openly and freely about their lives. The experience also encourages Forum members to develop world-class listening skills. It encourages them not to "solve" the problems they are hearing, but to relate, as appropriate, their own personal experiences that may give offer another way to see the dilemma.

Another member of our interdisciplinary team, J. Zink, a neuropsychotherapist and long time "resource" for YPO, has been invited to hundreds of Forum meetings as a guest moderator during the past 24 years. When he and Tom looked at the Forum model, both realized that with certain and very important modifications, the model could be the vehicle for creating the stress-reduced corporate climate our clients were seeking.

But we needed a different model. In the first place, we wanted to move away from a forum made up of peers from different—and non-competing—businesses. While this gives the members the freedom to discuss issues without fear of competitive repercussions, it offers little opportunity for the effects of the stress relief to filter throughout a single organization. Secondly, the use of a single (and minimally trained) "facilitator" has certain limitations. His or her role is only to keep the discussion rolling and balanced. Moreover, a mere facilitator may well fail to solve the most frequent problem in a group, the tendency to remain at a comfortable but often relatively shallow emotional level as the group considers issues in the lives of its members. And the experience is hard on the moderator. It is the equivalent of monitoring eleven therapy patients at the same time. It can be done, but it takes incredible concentration.

To address these issues, we decided that the Round Table would be composed of executives from a single company, and that all executives from the client company would participate. This modification accelerates the change in corporate culture that we were trying to create. Including colleagues from the same company also creates an on-going atmosphere of trust and authenticity that allows for emotional support on a daily basis. Furthermore, as we will discuss in a later chapter, the Round Table Journey can be successfully filtered down throughout the organization, dramatically accelerating the change as well as creating a common language and experience within the culture.

We also decided to include multiple moderators. In this way, we had more trained and experienced minds with additional sets of eyes and ears alert to the reality of what was building, transpiring, changing, and growing in the group. We believed—and have now proven—that having multiple experienced faculty moderators does in fact *guarantee initial success*. And that initial success is absolutely crucial to the potential for healing within a group.

And so the Round Table Journey began.

Our Thoughts

❖ Moderators are a team within the Round Table team.

❖ The Round Table model works well within a single company, helping to develop a healthy corporate culture.

Your Thoughts

1. Describe a Command & Control working or family environment you have experienced. What was it like? What were the results in that environment? How did you feel?

2. Describe the most trusting environment you have ever experienced, either professional or personal. What was it like? How did you feel?

TWO

Rule 1: Just Between Us Friends

Every subject's duty is the King's;
but every subject's soul is his own.

Henry V, Act IV, Scene I

The third member of our team, Jeffrey Zink, an Oxford-trained moral philosopher and ethicist, uses the phrase "lowering the sword and shield" to describe a process whereby a person becomes more authentic by speaking his or her own mind. As that great American philosopher, Marshal Matt Dillon, used to say on *Gunsmoke*, "Keep your eyes and ears open, do your own thinking, and be your own man." Well, it was a sexist age. But the Marshall's most excellent advice can be hard to follow in the highly competitive corporate world of relentless pressure to succeed.

The tendency to think like the boss or everybody else is very strong in many corporate environments. The logic is elegantly simple: If I think like either the boss or everyone else, I am safe. Many employees often equate termination of employment with death. They seem to carry this thought with them through the most mundane of corporate decisions. "What if I am wrong here? Could I be whacked for this?"

So, in part, the human need to fit in, to be part of the group, to avoid standing out, and to stay off unfriendly radar seems to originate with fear. And, as Freud explained to us, all fear is ultimately the fear of death.

Here, the sword and the shield are powerful images. We hide behind both. The shield protects us from the swords of others; our own sword can get in there and do its butcher work when called upon in order to ensure our survival. So we hide, and prepare, as T. S. Eliot said in *The Love Song of J. Alfred Pruefrock,* "a face to meet the faces that we meet."

Putting on a game face, raising the shield, and carrying a short but bloody sword seems to be the best way to survive the stressors of the Command & Control corporate world—a world, in the words of 17th Century philosopher Thomas Hobbes, that is "solitary, poor, nasty, brutish, and short."

The toll that this lifestyle can take on its practitioners is devastating. Many researchers have looked at the consequences of the stress levels in this life. Their clinical findings, well documented in the literature, include coronary diseases, alcoholism, chronic fatigue, depression, a variety of opportunistic cancers arising from a debilitated and compromised immune system, an ever-rising rate of divorce, and the litany of problems associated with the challenges of raising children.

Our interdisciplinary team did not set out to rid the world of these crushing realities. Ours was a more modest goal: Help corporate executives heal by giving them a place to go, on a regular basis, that would allow them to lower their swords and shields, for the luxury of an entire day, so that they might begin to practice a new lifestyle. It is a lifestyle that encourages them to be more open, freshly honest and candid, and as authentically truthful about their lives, past and present, as they could imagine themselves to be. We wanted to create an emotionally safe environment that would allow each of them the luxury of sharing their authentic thoughts and feelings. The research literature on this approach to the generalized anxiety caused by stress is also very clear: Just being able to talk about the stress dramatically relieves its symptoms.

Of course, we were aware that group therapy for executives is not new. But we were also aware that the limited success it enjoyed in the past was due to certain factors that seemed built into the typical executive personality. The real question always remained: How does one get power-centric, highly competitive, extremely well-educated, street smart, inordinately skeptical, financially accomplished, and often just plain shrewd individuals to take Marshal Dillon's advice *and share all of that thinking with the group?* The fundamental answer, of course, is stunningly simple: Create an atmosphere of trust. Research shows and common sense confirms that without the foundation of trust, the swords and shields stay fearfully in place.

Setting Up the Round Table

And so we needed a plan to create the trust—and in short order, since virtually none of the participants bring that into the room with them. Borrowing from the concept of the circle, which has its origins in sitting around the campfire telling stories, we structured the meeting room for the Round Table events by placing twelve to fifteen very comfortable chairs in a circle. Our little visual joke is that there is no round table in the Round Table. It is *imaginary*. In this way we get to see all of each other as we speak together. For executives accustomed to rectangular tables with pads of paper, pencils, water glasses, little mints, and a clear view of the PowerPoint slides, the set up of the Round Table room does stir some comment—and, no surprise, some anxiety.

Initially, if necessary, we use name tags, with first names only, written large enough so that they may be seen across the room. The meetings typically start at 8:00 a.m. sharp and we do not start until all those expected are in attendance or accounted for.

We ask that cell phones be turned off or switched to "stun" if someone has an emergency family situation brewing. Usually we sit down after breakfast together. Once the circle is complete, we remove any empty chairs and begin by reviewing the rules under which all Round Tables operate. We make it very clear that while we are flexible human beings, our Round Table rules are *not*. We operate this way to genially but firmly convey that what we are doing has a serious purpose and while none of us take ourselves too seriously, we do take our work seriously. This is an extremely important step in the building of trust.

Confidentiality

Our primary rule is absolute and total confidentiality. We explain that this means that no one in the Round Table may, at any time or for any reason, discuss with anyone, including other members of the Round Table, what was said by anyone in that room on that day. *The only*

exception to this is what members say about themselves.
This they are free to share with whomever they wish.

Then we seal the primary rule by having everyone in the circle raise his or her right hand. This symbolic gesture is important again in the building of trust. Once the hands go up, it is clear to everyone in the group that at least symbolically everyone else in the group has agreed to a bond of trust. Indeed, this is the real *origin of the trust* created in the group. If someone does not raise his or her hand, going any further in the process would be pointless. Should such a thing happen, the swords and the shields would raise automatically and we could have a really terrific discussion about the weather in Austin in July or the Dow in an election year. But not much else.

Our first rule is complete and total confidentiality.

In the Round Tables the three of us have experienced, which at this point includes nearly a thousand participants, we know of only one breach of confidentiality. Most people, we have found, take something as serious as raising their right hands in a purely symbolic gesture (no Bible, no oath) to be an affirmation of commitment. We recommend that a violation of confidentiality be considered grounds for expulsion from the group. Different groups may wish to handle this in their own fashion. This is okay; once the group is formed, then a modified democracy rules. More on this a little later.

One final note on the introduction of confidentiality to begin each Round Table: One of us always asks after the raising of the hands if anyone has any breaches of confidentiality to discuss. We ask this, obviously, from the second meeting of the Round Table going forward. If there are such breaches, we deal with them immediately and directly. The ensuing discussions themselves will generally bring the group together and whatever remedy the group agrees upon will constitute an object lesson for all that this process is serious. But almost always it has been our experience that there is nothing to discuss here. This, too, is a very important part in the trust building process. When everyone can look everyone else directly in the eyes and respond silently to an overt request for confidentiality breaches, then the group confidence in each other grows.

This growing confidence is one of the great powers inherent in the Round Table process.

Our Thoughts

❖ The Round Table offers a unique venue to unload pent-up stress.

❖ Confidentiality is the cornerstone of trust, and trust is the cornerstone of Round Table success.

Your Thoughts

1. Be honest: Do you put on a fake "game face" at work? At home? Why or why not?

2. How would you improve trust among the members of your team? In your family?

THREE

Rule 2: No Rank in the Round

> *. . . the valued file*
> *Distinguishes the swift, the slow, the subtle,*
> *The housekeeper, the hunter, every one,*
> *According to the gift which bounteous nature*
> *Hath in him clos'd; whereby he does receive*
> *Particular addition, from the bill*
> *That writes them all alike; and so of men.*

MacBeth, Act III, Scene I

The second rule for the Round Table concerns rank in the corporation and ego. As we review the rules during the start of each Round Table we remind all present that while he or she may be an Executive Vice President or Controller or Chairman of the Board at the company, in our Round Table meetings *no one holds any rank at all.* When we come together in this circle for the purpose of healing, we come only as the bright, creative, intuitive, well-educated, accomplished, sweet or sour, gentle or rough-hewn souls that God made us to be. We come there only as willing and attentive participants in the healing process; our purpose is to share our real lives—personal and professional—and listen with empathy as others share their lives with us.

We explain that our purpose is not to make everyone in the room more financially successful. In point of fact, we don't care whether they are making a lot of money or very little money at all. Money doesn't help us very much when we are dead. Our purpose is to create a group of helpful individuals who are unafraid to share the lives they have lived and are living. We explain that all of the fifteen or so members of the Round Table have lived a combined total of six hundred years or more. During that time on this earth, we have experienced a great deal of what life offers all of us. While no one is there to tell someone else how to live his or her life, it is very probable that someone in the group has faced the very situation that is troubling someone else in the group at that moment. It is also probable that this person has learned a great deal by living through this situation and has thoughts and feelings to share that may very well help someone else's own passage through a hard time.

We find the term, "touchy-feely" pretty funny.

It is usually at this time we point out that before people join one of our Round Tables and while reading a preliminary questionnaire we send out (reprinted at Chapter 15), they may well think, "Oh boy, here come the touchy-feely people!"

In response, we explain that one member of our team, Tom, started his career as president of one of the largest meat packing plants in Los Angeles. He began each day at 4:00 a.m. in cowboy boots and jeans while negotiating with truck driving teamsters. Another member of our team, Jeffrey, is a true American hero, who as a radar navigator-bombardier in the Strategic Air Command, had to jump out of a burning B-52. And the final member of our team, J., put himself through graduate school by driving a cab at night in the City of Detroit.

We find the term "touchy-feely" pretty funny.

All of which brings us to the subject of ego. The second part of Rule Two is that we ask all participants to leave their egos at the door. In Round Tables, just like in life, it is good to be humble.

As we listen to each other's stories we find out that there is a lot we didn't know about each other. We discover that we made a lot of things up about each other that simply were not true. We discover that we may have worked with someone for twenty years yet had no idea what happened to them in their childhood. Or how much it was like our own. We also discover that we have been judgmental when we might have been better served to get more information in the first place. Most importantly, we discover that our own egos often get in the way of a great deal of joy and wonderful satisfaction.

So there is no room in the room for egos and feelings of self importance. Indeed, time and again we see that *humility in the self* and *confidence in the group* empowers the Round Table members to share and learn from each other in a way that many find to be a completely singular experience in their lives.

Our second Round Table rule relieves everyone of his or her title and sense of entitlement. We don't want to know about titles or artificial respect; we want to know about the human being inside. We want to listen because each of us has something to give all of us—something we need. If we are listening politely to someone because of his or her rank in the company, we are doing so because we should. And "shoulds," we learn early, lead to unhealthy things. If we are listening politely because someone's ego demands that he or she dominate an entire morning, then we all are very glad this person is with us. He or she needs us more than others may.

We need everyone in the room. Because we often find as each person speaks, he or she has Hamlet's opportunity to listen to his or her own words and *grow emotionally because of what is being said.* There is often something enlightening to us as we each are given the uninterrupted opportunity to tell our story in our own words to an extremely focused and interested audience. Their ability to listen without judgment relieves us of the necessity to defend ourselves and allows us to evaluate our own situation more objectively. In transactional terms, it moves us from either our parent (blaming) or child (defending) ego state into our adult (sharing) ego state. This important emotional shift often permits us to do what we could not do before: To see ourselves as others may see us.

As many recent writers on the subject of emotional intelligence tell us, this is the intelligence over which we have the most ability to mature. This emotional growth lies at the very heart of the Round Table Journey.

Our Thoughts

❖ By listening non-judgmentally, we can learn a great deal from the experiences of the other sharing adults in the room.

❖ Egos and rank are barriers to trust and authenticity.

Your Thoughts

1. Think about the egos of the best leaders you have worked for. Think about the egos of the worst. Is there a correlation between ego and truly successful leadership?

2. On a scale of 1 to 10, evaluate your listening skills. Then ask your boss, a direct report, your life partner and your children (if any) to also rate your listening skills. How do the numbers compare?

FOUR

Rule 3: Check Your Weapons at the Door

One word more, one word.
This tiger-footed rage, when it shall find
The harm of unscann'd swiftness, will too late
Tie leaden pounds to 's heels. Proceed by process
Lest parties, as he is belov'd, break out
And sack great Rome with Romans.

Coriolanus, Act III, Scene I

Let us return to a consideration of the sword and the shield for a moment. We need to keep in mind that our defensive or offensive postures make the adult ego state (positive, open, sharing) virtually impossible to maintain. The sword, emblematic of the parent ego, cuts with the keen edge of criticism. Does any of this "parent" talk sound familiar?

"You did WHAT?"

"Come on! What were you thinking?"

"Idiots! I am surrounded by idiots!"

These and a thousand others come to mind immediately.

The shield, emblematic of the child ego, attempts to deflect the critical sword.

"Why do I always get the blame? I didn't do it!"

"He started it. It was his idea!"

"I was just doing what you told me to do in the first place!"

These exchanges, and thousands of others, begun long ago at home and now carried over into the workplace, are largely dysfunctional in both worlds.

Most executives know this. Only the truly inept find themselves shouting phrases like those above. The more clever practitioners of the art of verbal warfare have allowed their swords and shields to evolve into the thrust and parry of wit and humor. In the Round Table, we call humor at the expense of others a "zinger." And in Rule Number Three we move swiftly to take this version of sword and shield from the hands (mouths!) of our participants.

We define a zinger as anything said (including non-verbal communication) at the expense of another, even if it is hilarious (and it often is!). Because it ridicules the zingee, a zinger is a bad choice in the Round Table, and costs the "zinger slinger" $20. The money—in cash—goes on the floor in the middle of the Round Table where we all can see it for the remainder of our meeting.

When we introduce this rule we get a lot of questions. There is nothing like the prospect of the sudden loss of post-tax dollars to sharpen the minds of executives. The first question is always: "Who gets the money?"

We answer, "One of you is currently raising funds for a charitable cause. This money will go to that cause. Who wishes to be our banker?"

It has been axiomatic for us that there has been at least one executive *in every Round Table we have ever conducted* who was in the process of raising money for charity. All of our work has been with American executives and it has been said that Americans are the most generous people on the face of the earth. Our experience shows nothing to the contrary. We have had as many as five executives in the same Round Table actively engaged in raising money for a charity.

Next question: "Who decides whether what was said was a zinger or not?"

We answer: "The group. From now on the group makes all decisions that directly affect the group. The majority rules. We are, after all, a gloriously successful democracy."

Next question: "What if I zing myself? Can I take back twenty bucks?"

We answer: "No. But zinging yourself is not only permitted, it is encouraged. We see self-zinging as a sign of sound mental health and elegant humility."

In the course of our Round Tables to date, we have raised over $15,000 for a variety of charitable causes that include the American Diabetes Association, Muscular Dystrophy, Shelters for Abused Women and Children, and so on.

The reason why the No-Zinger rule is so important is that we have found that most executives were raised in highly competitive environments. They learned early how to attack and defend themselves with their wit. By taking these weapons away from them, we help them to more carefully monitor their mouths. For often what they say is a matter of sheer habit. Raised in a verbal kill or be killed environment, they often "shoot" without thinking. And they can be oblivious to the emotional pain their wit can inflict on others—especially those who work for them and their spouses and children.

The $20 zinger rule has been incredibly effective for us in teaching our executives how to control their tongues and begin to take responsibility for the words they use in communicating with others. After the rule of confidentiality, we consider our $20 zinger rule to be our most effective rule at *being* the change we wish to create.

There can be no question that American men especially have learned to communicate affection through verbal abuse. But this zinger-slinger culture often keeps us from communicating our true feelings. Or from feeling very much at all. Many double blind and very scientific research studies have shown repeatedly that people who repress their feelings are at serious risk for a variety of opportunistic diseases.

The zinger rule has helped teach executives to take responsibility for the words they use.

It is so very healthy (not to mention stress relieving) to laugh deeply and freely, to feel the emptiness of sadness and just cry, or to openly express our affections and love.

Finding our feelings and honoring them through genuine and authentic expression can be one of the most stress reducing activities for us. The zinger rule works for this important and unique reason: Because even when the zingers are flying and the cash is hitting the floor, the laughter is evenly divided between the zinger and the zingee. It is this shift that helps to set the stage for the personal revelations to come.

Our Thoughts

❖ Verbal shots, even funny ones, damage or destroy group trust.

❖ The No-Zinger rule can be exported out of the Round Table and into daily work with very successful results.

Your Thoughts

1. Are there times when zingers are healthy?

2. Have you worked or lived in an environment that was poisoned by constant zinging? Have you had a zinging parent or a zinging boss? If so, what were the repercussions?

FIVE

Rule 4: Try to See It My Way

Such welcome and unwelcome things at once;
'Tis hard to reconcile.

MacBeth, Act IV, Scene III

Our final rule for conducting a successful Round Table concerns dissent. Traditionally one dissents in a corporate environment at some, and sometimes great, peril. It is often extremely difficult to stand up and tell your boss that she or he is wrong. In a Command & Control environment such a statement can be read as insubordination. You may be viewed as a "loose cannon" or "out of step," or "off the reservation," (all military metaphors). Sometimes openly disagreeing with the boss in front of other employees is actually greeted with shock by everyone. There can be a dreadful stillness in the room as everyone comes to red alert just to see how you are going to die.

After all, agreeing with the boss is a time honored tradition. "She is right; that is why she's the boss," the thinking goes. Or, "Hey, he signs the checks."

Well, bosses make mistakes. Perhaps company-killing mistakes. Sometimes going along with the boss can get you a federal indictment. Just ask former Enron CFO Andrew Fastow.

In our Round Tables, we celebrate dissent. We expect it; we honor it; and we are disappointed when we do not get it. The reasons why we enjoy dissent make perfect sense to everyone once we explain them. Research studies on group dynamics repeatedly show that a lone dissenting voice raises issues that the group must face. In facing a dissenting opinion, the group must work through things more deeply. Often the group arrives at a much different place after considering the thinking of the dissenting voice. More importantly, the group *learns because of it.* This learning is growth for the group. It takes place in an atmosphere of trust where swords and shields are lowered. The ensuing dialectic makes the group work through new thinking on a given subject. It bonds the group by giving it new skills, often a new "language of dissent," and the confidence that comes from facing difficult issues and plotting a new course to account for varying views on a given subject.

The group learns and grows because of the dissenting voice.

Here is where we have found that ethnic, geographic, or gender diversity greatly enhances the Round Table Journey. An African American woman executive raised by a single mother in a Detroit ghetto will usually have a different take on things than a room full of tobacco-dipping good ol' boy engineers from Georgia. The group discovers that it grows because of the inputs from all points of view.

When we say "celebrate," we mean it. When someone says, "With all due respect, I have to push back from the way the group is seeing this issue. I see it another way," *we lead the applause!* Members of the Round Table quickly learn that dissent, as Thomas Jefferson said of rebellion, "now and then is a good thing."

But, of course, there is dissent and there is dissent. From the point of view of the parent-child conflict, which is the principal logical outcome of the Command & Control style of management, dissent can turn the Table into a debating society. This may polarize the group, be tiresome and largely unproductive, and keep things testy, on-edge, and possibly ugly.

Here is a recommendation for that situation: The moderator says something like this, "Well, I suppose we could debate that all day and still not get anywhere. Let's agree to move on." Then he or she follows this immediately with a question about feelings—because there can be no argument about one's authentic feelings.

What Jeffrey has called "Management by Relationship," we see as the most effective cure for the parent-child conflict that results from a management style of Command & Control. Management by Relationship only happens when all of the company associates see themselves as partners in the enterprise and work to create an environment where adults exchange information and offer support for the general good of the enterprise and all of the people engaged in it. J. has coined the phrase, "ferocious cooperation." This shared sense of emotional support leads to what our dear friend and great life coach, Dr. Larry Wilson calls "becoming the company that if it existed would put your company out of business." It is a truly worthwhile goal, if, in the process of doing this, you create an environment of support, cooperation, and plain old fun. Then the stress of Command & Control is replaced by the *eustress* (healthy stress) of being "in the zone" of healthy achievement.

We believe that the Round Table, complete with its Rules of Engagement, is the first step toward becoming that wonderfully healthy workplace. Because when the Round Tables meet in an atmosphere of complete trust (the rule of confidentiality and the rule of no ego and no rank) to gain acceptance and understanding (the rule of no zingers) for the purpose of improving the emotional health of the individuals (the rule of encouraging dissent), then some fairly astonishing things begin to happen to the executives in the room.

For openers, they begin to behave like healthy, authentic human beings. And they start to become really good friends. That alone is a powerfully healthy, adult experience that the parent-child conflict stifles.

For, as most of us know, few things in life are better for you than good friends. Good friends do not tell you how to live your life (parent). They do not make judgments about your choices (parent). Good friends know how to share their emotions and face adversity together (adult). If you really do have to go to war, it is very comforting to know that you can count on the person next to you. Because she or he can count on you.

Our Thoughts

❖ The dissenting voice is one of the ways we see the adult ego in action.

❖ Honoring the dissenting voice is an important sign of an emotionally healthy group.

❖ Dissent forces a group to re-examine and refine its thinking.

Your Thoughts

1. How is dissent normally greeted in your workplace? In your family?

2. If dissent is not welcomed, what strategies could you use to change that?

3. How do your relationships with your friends differ from your relationships with you co-workers? With your family members?

Part II: Living It

SIX

Open for Business

> *. . . Counterfeit? I lie, I am no counterfeit.*
> *To die is to be a counterfeit, for he is but the*
> *counterfeit of a man who hath not the life of a man;*
> *But to counterfeit dying, when a man thereby liveth,*
> *is to be no counterfeit, but the true and perfect*
> *image of life indeed.*

Henry IV First Part, Act V, Scene V

One of the most important features of the Round Table is authenticity. Getting executives to open their hearts as well as their minds and begin to share their own lives as they truly see them can be a great challenge. Even with the emotionally safe environment that the rules of the Round Table were crafted to create, engendering an atmosphere of trust and emotional support can be challenging.

As moderators, our task is to create that special environment. Over the years we have developed a rather unique skill set to accomplish this. As the Round Table begins, it must be clear to all who sit in the circle that this is serious work. One of us reviews the rules of the Round Table, which we do at the start of every session.

Assuming for purposes of this discussion that all the rules have been presented or reviewed and no breach of confidentiality has been reported, the question then presents itself:

Now what do we do?

Executives generally are uncomfortable with a meeting that appears to have no agenda. This is why American executives love a pre-printed agenda to match the presentations, complete with the ubiquitous PowerPoint.

Still, as a moderator, you may think that, in the interest of efficiency, it would be a good idea to send out some sort of agenda about the questions or exercises you plan to introduce. But we caution you, as you prepare each Round Table session, do not tip your hand and distribute the questions (or topics or any sort of agenda) prior to the meeting. One of the truly beautiful and effective experiences of the Round Table is its spontaneity.

As moderators for the Round Table, we know that our true purpose is "deal with what emerges," and to follow where that emerging reality takes us. This is the very essence of a psychotherapeutically sound approach. The members of the Round Table must ultimately feel that they are free to speak their minds so that they and the group may discover where their heads and their hearts are.

"Tell us something about yourself that the group doesn't know."

Getting to this place of safety is a process. It does not happen because of a certain special set of circumstances and words that are spoken in a certain way. But when the rules of the Round Table are presented in a calm, positive, serious, and well-measured voice, the tone of the meeting has been set. This tone, never sarcastic, disrespectful, or overly dramatic, is essential to the process. It can be light, intelligent, sensitive and humorously self-deprecating, or business-like and straight-forward, but it must convey the feeling that we are embarking on a journey of discovery.

Perhaps the best exercise we know to begin the journey works like this: We ask, on a *volunteer basis only*, for someone to tell us two things about him or herself that the group does not now know, one professional and one personal, so that we as a group might get to know him or her better.

If members of the Round Table seem uncomfortable with the request, one of us will volunteer to go first. What follows then is an honest and open sharing by one of us regarding his own life. All three of us have led interesting lives and we have some good and quite revealing—and painful—stories to tell. This self-disclosure, we have found, almost certainly gives a great deal of permission for others to speak. Actually, it is quite rare for a group of executives to remain quiet for long. Most are quite willing to share their lives, accomplishments, and failures. This turns out to be true especially if they have suffered a great deal, whether by circumstance or their own bad choices.

The important thing here is that someone speaks and begins to share his or her life with the group. This gets everyone past a great deal of anxiety.

The stories generally fall into the category of "I bet you don't know this about me," and contain a variety of real-life experiences. These include firings, divorces, health problems, unique previous employment, aberrant parent stories, sibling horror stories, extended responsibility stories (taking care of other people's children, adoptions, sick relatives and friends, etc.), and recounting things that happened that generally resulted because of the failings of others in their lives.

After the first speaker completes his or her monologue, it is important that we as moderators ask short but pertinent questions regarding parts of the presentation that might need clarification. This must never sound like a cross-examination. These are gentle requests for further information. If the speaker gets the feeling that we are earnestly seeking to understand the situation, she or he will be encouraged to share more information.

At this point, we often turn to the group and ask if someone has a question or can share an observation about what we have just heard. *This is extremely important.* We do not want to exclude the members of the group in any way. If we fail to encourage them to make observations or ask questions about what they have just heard, then this experience devolves into a therapy session between the speaker and the moderators. While there are times when that does happen, and with good reason, these opening sharings are generally not the place to allow this kind of specialized dialogue to occur.

Sometimes the opening sharing lasts less than ten minutes. If that happens, it is okay. Generally speaking, time is not important and we shy from setting any kind of time limit at all. Naturally, if a filibuster begins and we get the feeling that after twenty minutes or more that our speaker is just warming up, one of us might say something like, "We do have many more people to speak, so we might want to save some of this good stuff for consideration later," but this almost never happens.

It is of the utmost importance that the entire group gets the message that we are here for the purpose of listening intently to what is being said (hence the courtesy of turning off cell phones and Blackberries). The very fact that a group of powerful and time-conscious executives would stop the progress of their lives for the purpose of focusing on one person sends a strong message of high regard to the speaker. Later, as we get to the deeper levels of communication, this support of the group will develop into a first-class stress reducer, although this, of course, is not true generally the first time one speaks to the group. Often this first time sharing is accompanied by the typical stress one feels speaking in front of a group of one's peers or one's boss.

We always thank the speaker by applause. One of us will say, "We certainly want to thank Julie for sharing these parts of her life and the sheer courage to speak first. Let's thank her for her leadership." Then we applaud with vigor and enthusiasm. Half-hearted applause is really worse than no applause and should be avoided.

Once the first speaker has concluded, the jitters of expectation will greatly subside in the group. We can see in most of the eyes the feeling that "Well, that wasn't so bad after all."

It wasn't. And it only gets better.

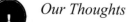

Our Thoughts

❖ The open agenda allows the group to deal with what emerges.

❖ Sharing one's authentic life story with a group of friends is very healthy.

❖ Members of the Round Table should be encouraged and challenged, but never forced, to speak.

Your Thoughts

1. When are you most allowed to just be you at work? At home?

2. How do you react to tears, your own or someone else's? Are you comfortable with a display of emotions?

3. Let's go deep: Where do you get your strength today? Has that changed over the course of your life?

SEVEN

Adults Only, Please

Where is my other life? Mine own is gone.

Henry VI First Part, Act IV, Scene VII

When the first speaker is applauded for revealing some things about his or her life, the initial tone is set. At the telling of these first stories, much is going on in the minds of the members of the group.

Executives tend to gather information that can help them with their lives and careers. Here before them is an opportunity that is fairly rare. In the first place, they sit transfixed by what they are hearing. They are learning something about someone with whom they have worked, often for many years, that they did not know. Furthermore, because there is a relatively limited number of human stories, the odds are great that they know someone with a similar story, or it well may be that the story before them has obvious parallels to their own lives. In either case, the experience is compelling. There are few more engrossing human activities than listening to someone you thought you knew tell a previously unknown story that has powerful similarities to your own.

This begins the "drawing in" experience that is quintessential to the Round Table Journey. Members of the Round Table who have similar experiences to the stories told are strongly encouraged, by the very nature of the stories, to reveal their own. This is not in the spirit of "if you think that is so bad, wait until you hear this one," although with poor moderation skills, that can happen. (We have included a set of skills that effective moderators possess. See Chapter 12.) More probably, the "drawing in" will result in a greater and immediate group intimacy in which the clear message is simple: It is okay to share your stress and pain here. We will listen without judgment.

By the time the second or third member has spoken, this non-judgmental tone should be pervasive throughout the circle of trust. If it is not, then the moderators have not really done their jobs. In transactional terms, "parent" and "child" responses are inappropriate as the sharing continues; the only conceivably effective responses are "adult."

We will listen without judgment.

To be specific: The "parent" response seeks to judge, condemn, or even ridicule. Not always by verbal cues, but by non-verbals as well (soft whistles of surprise, groans, head shaking, eyes rolling, hands suddenly up-raised) can give the speaker and the group the sense that the person in his or her "parent" disapproves of what is being said or has a much better solution than the one being shared.

The most damaging part of the "parent" is the need to fix it. What gets damaged is the relationship between the speaker and the person in the "parent" ego state. "Fixing" the problem is just about the last thing the group needs to consider. The only time "fixing" is appropriate is when the speaker directly asks for help. But this happens only after deep trust has been carefully crafted and the members of the Round Table have learned "adult" responses.

One of our most fundamental principles in the Round Table is that no adult has the right to tell another adult how she or he "ought to" or "should" behave. This principle is often difficult for executives to grasp. But understand the underlying meaning: When I try to fix your problem for you, I am saying, in part, you are not capable of fixing it yourself. This is denigrating and destructive in a relationship, whether it is with a co-worker, a life partner or a child. While *you* can say you're not able to fix it, I do not have the right to say or imply that.

Executives generally think of themselves as "fix it" people. Self-described "problem solvers," executives love to hear (at least part!) of the problem, recognize it to be one they have solved before, and fire out a bulletized list of steps leading to "Done!"

Some executives who have done this to their life partners quickly learn that they want them to distinguish between "solve" and "listen." Invariably partners need "listen" far more than they need "solve."

We all deeply crave emotional healing. We need other human beings to sit and listen while we tell of our troubling circumstances. Just being able to talk to someone who listens without judgment or advice is a healing experience in itself.

The very first Round Tables, with all due respect to King Arthur and his knights, were held nightly around campfires by our ancestors who had completed the day's hunting, gathering, and/or farming. As they ate, they shared their stories. Telling and listening to these stories created in us a powerfully therapeutic experience that we all crave to this day. But in our techno-society, we eat on the run and rarely as a family around the same table any more. We sit in our sterile cubicles with pictures of our family members as guilty reminders that these people do exist. We just do not see them as often as we need to. For them and for us.

And instead of face-to-face and heart-to-heart meetings at the campfire, we now communicate with each other by cell phone while driving in our mobile cubicles. Or by thumbing emails on the run while waiting to get into flying cubicles traveling at nearly the speed of sound.

It is this new identity that allows the transformation from the isolated "I" to the recognition of "WE."

It is a common executive experience to ask: "Why am I doing this to myself?"

As each person begins to tell his or her tale, the Round Table takes on a genuine feeling of warmth, acceptance, and understanding. This begins to bond the group into a new identity. It is this new identity that allows the transformation from the isolated "*I*" to the recognition of "*WE*."

The "WE" begins to form because the group discovers that we are all suffering to one extent or another, that we have all had doubts about our lives and the choices we have made, that we all struggle with our children, that our children all struggle mightily with us, that we all experience astonishingly similar thoughts and feelings that can downright torture us unless we have the skills to reframe our experiences, that many of us walk around with open wounds caused by "the slings and arrows of outrageous fortune," and that each of us carries a potential gift for another: Medicine for the wounds.

It has been our almost sacred experience that *individuals* walk into a Round Table in the morning but a *team* walks out at the end of the day.

Our Thoughts

❖ Emotional healing takes place when people listen without judgment.

❖ Authenticity and the willingness to share transforms a group of individuals into a team.

Your Thoughts

1. What is your own definition of Team?

2. Be honest, again: Do you interact with people in your life more in the "parent" mode, the "child" mode, or the "adult" mode?

3. Think about the one adult in your childhood who had the most positive impact on your development. What mode was he or she in?

EIGHT

Should Is a Four-Letter Word

O, the fierce wretchedness that glory brings us!
Who would not wish to be from wealth exempt,
Since riches point to misery and contempt?

Timon of Athens, Act IV, Scene II

Much has been written in recent years about the tyranny
of the word "should." It, and others like it, "ought," "have
to," "had better," are preponderantly parent words. Telling
someone what they "should" do, especially when they do
not seek advice from us, tends to drive them to the place
of the defensive child. Resenting the judgment, fearing
condemnation and rejection, the child strikes back with all
the defense mechanisms nature gives us: counter-attack,
manipulations, emotional exploitation, and the struggles
of verbal pyrotechnics. None of these consequences of the
parent-child struggles is good. Unfortunately, these
consequences are the inevitable side-effects of Command
& Control management.

"My way or the highway," isn't in the same song as "take
this job and shove it," but it *should* be.

We have observed in our many Round Tables that today's
executives, in their late forties and early fifties, and
mostly all "raised" in the Command & Control leadership
style, are learning that their direct reports, in their thirties
and early forties, do not respond well to this management
style.

Young executives today have many more choices than their parents did in the corporate world. They are very mindful of their own mobility. The best and the brightest of them realized that they could get sick from the stress caused by an overbearing, hard-charging, chainsaw-wielding boss. They saw their parents' generation lose their marriages, become disaffected from their children, and ultimately lose their health because of the deleterious effects of their own workaholism.

These rising stars are refusing to give their lives for the well-being of anonymous institutional investors. They are paying attention to things like working conditions, special benefits, flex-time, and being part of a cohesive team.

Here's another way to look at the disconnect between the differing thought processes of some senior executives and their junior protégés: "Should" is, in the words of the 18th Century philosopher, Immanuel Kant, a "hypothetical imperative." Simply put, "*If* you want to be where I am in the corner office, then you *should* do these things." But the problem with a hypothetical imperative is that it only works if the person being addressed actually wants the stuff after the "if." Otherwise, the statement has no power. "If you want x, then you should do y" won't motivate me to do y if I don't care about getting x. And many junior executives today are deciding that the personal costs of doing y are too high.

So "should" begins to lose its commanding power when those to whom it was so often directed hear it as a clinical sign of illness rather than a directional indication.

One of the most energizing aspects of our Round Tables is discovering that the oppressiveness of "should" remains a vestige of an unhealthy management style. The Round Table directly addresses stress in the workplace by recommending that all of our participants read Dr. Danny Baker's elegant assault on unhealthy executive stress titled *What Happy People Know*. In addition, we have them read Dr. J. Zink's *Ego States* and Dr. Jeffrey Zink's *Choices*. These three books, plus Dr. Taylor Hartman's *The Color Code* and our own *From I to WE,* constitute the core curriculum of the Round Table. You **should** read them (just kidding!).

The human organism tends to fall into the same traps over and over again.

As speaker after speaker shares his or her story and the stories echo familiar themes and issues, the group begins to realize that for all of their dissimilar backgrounds and even ethnic and cultural diversities, the human organism clearly tends to fall into the same traps over and over again. These traps are thoroughly documented in the reference books above.

But while some of the executives in the Round Table may find themselves struggling against the steel teeth of one of these traps, other executives sitting right in front of them may well have been in those traps before. Co-dependency, alcoholism, angry teenage children, contentious ex-spouses, shifting markets, onerous governmental regulation, ever-expanding information technology, inter-departmental warfare, aging parents, lost children, dysfunctional childhoods, etc., become the issues before the group. And twelve to fifteen intelligent, well-educated, empathetic, and life-experienced minds react to the speaker.

Please note: This reaction is not to tell her or him what *should* be done in this situation, but to share what has happened in their own similar situations. This sharing is for the purpose of explaining their own outcomes when they faced this circumstance. It is adult-to-adult information exchange at its finest.

This collective experience bonds the group like few other human experiences. One of our faculty team lost his wife at a relatively young age. When he tells this story, often we discover that others in the group have lost a spouse. Their response to his story creates an immediate bond of friendship and understanding between the two widowers that is more easily felt than described. And each can draw wisdom from the other's walk through hell, while the rest of the group grapples with their inevitable future loss.

Traditionally, and especially in the old Command & Control style of management, the prevailing wisdom was to keep one's work life and home life separate. Thus, co-workers could co-exist beside each other for twenty years and not know that each other had suffered under an alcoholic parent. For one thing, technology has served to powerfully blur the lines between home life and work life. Now executives call each other all times of the day and night. Their ubiquitous cell phones ring at little league games, piano recitals, grocery stores, and even during bathroom trips.

Learning about another person's real life away from work often teaches powerful respect and a greater understanding of this person and his or her life struggles. That empathy, rare in powerful and achievement-motivated executives, can create a team understanding and cohesiveness that relieves an extraordinary amount of work-related tension and stress.

Danny Baker points out in *What Happy People Know* that the flight or fight response in us is directly responsible for dumping powerful chemicals (cortisol, adrenaline, norepinephrine, etc.) into our bloodstreams which, unused by fleeing or fighting, can begin, over time, to powerfully degrade our immune systems and result in the invasion of opportunistic cancers in our lymph and other vital systems.

At about this point, the group begins to recognize that we have all concocted some fairly unhealthy executive lifestyles. More importantly, they realize that, *as a leadership team,* we can begin to make better choices for ourselves, our families, and our co-workers. And from this realization begins to emerge the powerful concept of positive *groupthink.*

It has been clinically proven in study after double-blind study that no single individual can consistently out-think the group. But the group has to be a group. Until the group begins to bond emotionally, and trust one another, it is just a bunch of people who work for the same company. At that point it doesn't take a Thomas Jefferson or an Alexander Hamilton to outthink them. But the research shows that an emotionally bonded, trusting group can successfully tackle even the most vexing problem. That is because a group of trusted individuals can think aloud and brain-storm without fear of ridicule or rejection.

Study after study reports that the most powerful and compelling motivator of executives in the workplace is to belong to a team engaged in creating something bigger than themselves and making a solid contribution to the enterprise.

Perhaps the single most dramatic example of positive, creative *groupthink* occurred in Mission Control on April 13, 1970, during the flight of Apollo 13, in the wake of astronaut Jack Swigart's ominous under-statement: "OK, Houston, we've had a problem."

In the ensuing 86 hours and 57 minutes (three days), scores of left-brained (analytic) engineers and scientists across the country, spearheaded by the pocket-protector team in Mission Control and of course the crew of Apollo 13, whose veins ran with ice (which actually matched the 38-degree temperature inside the command module on the trip home), furiously exercised their right brains to invent solution after creative solution to the mounting problems of three men in a can 200,000 miles from home. Tenacity, resourcefulness, out of the box thinking and just plain guts ruled the day—and productive, effective *groupthink* solved the most challenging rescue problem in human history.

A group of trusted individuals can think aloud and brain-storm without fear of ridicule or fear of rejection.

This is where the positive *groupthink* of the Round Table excels. What a great human joy it is to witness a group of talented and creative executives thinking and feeling their way through a challenging problem. The stories of Microsoft, General Electric, The Skunk Works, Apple Computer, and the Whiz Kid days of the Ford Motor Company all inspire us with exquisite examples of *groupthink*.

A healthy, emotionally bonded group agrees to not attack an idea that strikes them as unproductive; it agrees to just move on to ones that are productive—this is the essence of "ferocious cooperation." It is the highest level to which the adult ego can aspire. In this situation, *stress* becomes *eustress.* As Danny Baker explains, this is when the energy inside the body is used in an entirely productive (and not frustrated) manner. This is what athletes call being *in the zone.* There is no healthier place to be. It is why exercise, which *uses up* the chemicals our stressed bodies are producing, is so good for us. And it is why sitting in traffic, late for a terribly important meeting that we wanted to avoid in the first place begins to kill us.

But when you can work with people you trust—and know they have your best interests at heart—amazing things can happen. There is a story of ferocious cooperation that takes place at a Midwestern county fair, where contests are held to see which draft horse can pull the heaviest load. In one such contest, the winning horse pulled a sled with 4,500 pounds. The second-place winner managed to drag 4,000 pounds. When the contest was over, the owners got together (no doubt over a couple of beers) and speculated about what they could do to get the second-place horse to pull a heavier load. They decided to harness them together and load up another sled. Together, the two horses pulled not 8500 or even 9000 pounds—they pulled 12,000 pounds, 3500 pounds more than they could pull alone. Call it *groupthink*. Call it synergy. The power of the group is nothing short of amazing.

What about companies who ignore this power? In his book, *Choices,* Dr. Jeffrey Zink describes companies who failed to understand that building relationships among employees ultimately costs the corporation dearly. Sometimes it costs the corporation its own existence.

Reducing unhealthy stress and emotionally connecting employees is only the beginning of the corporate uses to which Round Table principles can be applied. A group of bonded, sensitive and talented adults who understand that the game is not competing with each other but competing with the rest of the world is indeed a formidable force.

They become the company that if it existed would put the company they used to be out of business.

And there is nothing *should* about it.

Our Thoughts

❖ Positive *groupthink* (using the collective wisdom of the group) is a powerful tool for evoking latent creativity.

❖ In a healthy person, "What *should* I do?" is replaced with "What works best for me?" In a healthy family or company, "What *should* we do?" is replaced with "What works best for all of us?"

Your Thoughts

1. When are you at your creative best? How can you increase those moments?

2. Are you emotionally rewarded or punished for thinking creatively?

3. Is the atmosphere in your current workplace characterized by internal competition or cooperation?

4. Which of the members of your team or your family bring out your creative best? Why? How do they do it?

NINE

MBR: Management By Relationship

Ill-weav'd ambition, how much thou art shrunk!
When that this body did contain a spirit,
A kingdom for it was too small a bound;
But now two paces of the vilest earth
Is room enough.

Henry IV First Part, Act V, Scene IV

We have discovered that, among other things, the Round Table does away with the most negative aspects of Command & Control management. It provides a truly democratic and safe place to express views that may not be popular to the prevailing corporate hierarchy. It also provides a safe place to discover how close or far one's own views are from the real thinking of one's colleagues, instead of "the company line."

This is nothing but healthy. For, just like individuals, when a company's head and heart are at odds, then a lot of unhealthy things begin to happen. People are forced to live the lives of double agents. Often the disparity between what I think and what I am supposed to think forces me into the stressful position of filtering out my true thoughts and feelings that I need to express some way in order to stay healthy.

Repeated studies demonstrate how the disparity between head and heart is not only unhealthy, it decimates individual initiative and creativity.

One thing about the human organism is certain: Negative feelings that are repressed, placed as it were in shoeboxes on the shelf of some neurological closet, will find their way out. When they do, more often than not, they present themselves in the unpleasant form of destructive behaviors. Drug and alcohol abuse, destructive sexual escapades, ethical corner-cutting, company theft, spousal abuse, depression, and other anger-based behaviors are often the result of repressed emotions. What usually happens in companies today is that these aberrant behaviors are either excused or over-looked, especially when the executive in question is a "proven performer." If he or she isn't, and often after some major crisis, this person is just let go.

These common destructive behaviors and the company's reactive policy to them are part of a general picture of some corporate life today. As one executive said to us, "We get them in here, take their best years, use their best ideas, and basically throw them away." Or, as another put it, "Praise? You want praise for your work? You see that check every two weeks? There's your praise!"

By contrast, the Round Table introduces a distinctively different management approach—MBR: Management by Relationship. As typified by our work in the Round Table, MBR sends a remarkably different message to employees. It says this: "You are our most precious asset. We care enough about you as a person to create and maintain an emotionally healthy environment in which you can work. We are proactive about doing preventative work to maintain that environment for you and the members of your team. From time to time, we will give you opportunities for emotional growth and personal development because we know you are here for the purpose of supporting your family. Here, God and family come before our bottom line. And while the bottom line is important, because without it, we could not go forward, it is not the most important thing. Our values are the rudder by which we steer this ship. And we value you."

The Round Table Journey allows executives to actively bring those lofty values and mission statements into alignment with "the way things really are." In the words of Jeffrey, "There is no healthier thing you can do for your employees than to actually live by your stated values."

As one of our most cherished clients, the CEO of a six billion dollar, Fortune 500 company, said to a recent meeting of his top executive team, "Make no mistake. This is no country club. We all work very, very hard here. But we will only achieve success by doing the right thing."

There is no healthier thing you can do for your employees than to actually live by your stated values.

As our executives in the Round Tables begin to have at least a half dozen or so experiences with the model, it starts to occur to them that they are acquiring the skills necessary to moderate their own Round Tables for their direct reports and their teams—the skills of MBR. We encourage this thinking by often commenting on the process as well as the subject matter before the Table. Teaching the process by example, and being fully integrated members of each Table by not only moderating but telling our own stories and opening up our own lives as well, we have found a general enthusiasm among our members for conducting their own Round Tables. This ingrains the process of MBR deeper into the organization. It has been said in a variety of ways that true change inevitably comes from the grass roots up and that leaders are those who can spot a moving train and best figure out how to take their passage in the locomotive.

But we define leadership this way: A leader is the opposite of a victim. He or she is a person who takes other people to places that they could not go by themselves.

One of the continuing surprises of our Round Tables is that the leaders who emerge in the process of taking people from unhealthy thinking to healthier and more realistic ways of thinking and behaving *are not always those who have been singled out by the company as its most promising leaders*. Sometimes they are, for sure. But other times we are awe-struck by the profound moral courage and leadership it takes to sit calmly and share the true story of what happened in the past.

Here is another way to see what happens in a Round Table and the development of MBR: There are, in essence, four levels of response to the question, "Hi. How are you doing?"

- Level I is completely superficial: "Fine. Things are great. Thanks for asking." This is often our level at the office. It's a lie, but we all share in that lie.

- Level II is a little deeper: "I've been better. Nothing serious; I'll get through it." A little more honesty here, but still pretty close to the emotional vest.

- Level III begins to open some doors: "Actually I'm having some problems with my teenage son. Not unusual, I guess, but still it's pretty challenging." This level requires a fairly significant component of trust not needed at the other levels.

- Level IV is where deep sharing takes place: "Not so good. I just found out my son is snorting cocaine. I am out of my league here, and I need help." At this deepest level of communication, we see a bond of trust and connection that is soul to soul.

It has been our consistent joy in the Round Table that, time after time, the members get to Level IV communication *on the very first day*. This is truly remarkable until you realize that the whole purpose of the Round Table Journey is to get people to that place—and how much they yearn to be there. For that is where true trust is secured and real stress relief takes place. In the process of reaching Level IV, we discover an executive's true leadership skills. Here we are most authentic and able to meet and develop meaningful relationships with other authentic human beings.

Our Thoughts

❖ MBR breaks down Command & Control barriers and releases the creative energy of the most talented people.

❖ MBR is the practical application of genuine respect for another human being.

Your Thoughts

1. Can you bring the lessons and practices of the Round Table into your home? How would you do that? What would it feel like?

2. Another opportunity to be honest: Do the people you work with believe that you manage by relationship? How well do you know the people who work with you? What specifically can you do to learn more about them?

TEN

Stress Test

Canst thou, O partial Sleep, give thy repose
To the wet sea-boy in an hour so rude,
And in the calmest and most stillest night,
With all appliances and means to boot,
Deny it to a king? Then happy low, lie down!
Uneasy lies the head that wears the crown.

Henry IV Second Part, Act III, Scene I

In actuality, at the first Round Table with a given group there is only one exercise: Each member tells a part of his or her life story in answer to the question, "*Tell us one thing we do not know about you personally and one thing we do not know about you professionally.*" But the real anxiety, at least for moderators, comes in the follow-on sessions: What do we do for an encore?

We recommend that a newly formed Round Table meet on a monthly basis, at least for the first six months. The first session, with its personal revelations, is a great start, but the second and subsequent sessions are critical. The bonding that takes place during this time achieves the goal of building trust and deep relationships among the members. This goal is accomplished when the members look forward with genuine anticipation to each Round Table. Indeed, it has been our experience that when we transition to meeting every other month, the members complain about going so long between sessions. That alone proves that these are not typical business meetings.

So what do you do in the second session? There are a number of exercises you can consider for kicking off the day (See Chapter 14), but one highly effective tool for solidifying the group is the Stress Test.

The Stress Test works like this: "*If we could represent your unhealthy stress number on a scale of one to ten, with ten being the worst stress you have ever experienced and one being little or no stress at all, what is your number right now? Also, tell us whether that number is rising, falling, or holding steady. And tell us why.*"

This simple exercise, with, again, volunteers to speak, creates powerful discussion points for the Round Tables going forward. Even with only ten or twelve members of a given Table, the toughest part of the day will be having enough time for all who wish to speak.

The stress "barometer" is a revelationary experience. It is especially insightful to learn whether the group's numbers are falling or rising. The stress number gives us a snapshot of the stress in our lives, but the barometer reading reveals trends that are often hidden, even to the individual: Knowing that my number is rising can alert me to lurking dangers. Conversely, realizing that my number is falling *in and of itself* relieves some of my stress, since I can begin to see the proverbial light at the end of the tunnel.

The test also serves this function: When speaker after speaker reports his or her stress number at 8 or 9 and rising, the group begins to discover what we have done to ourselves as human beings. Some of us, in order to feed, clothe, and house our families, are writing checks that our bodies cannot cash. There is a price, often ugly and steep, to pay for living for the future at the expense of the present. We promise ourselves that it will get better next month or next year only to find that when we get there that it is actually worse: The current stress times become "the good old days."

Of course, there are times when we all have to work hard and long hours to achieve something special, but when twelve and fourteen hour days become a lifestyle, then we are overriding the feedback of the human organism. It is axiomatic in our profession that we see the bad choices of our 20's, 30's, and 40's often must be paid for in the 50's. Statistically, it is a rough decade of life. Those of us who have buried close friends in their 50's often have those quiet graveside talks with each other about "the golden years" that never happened for some.

The studies on work habits show conclusively a degradation of performance beyond eight continuous hours of extended work. This makes those hours expensive in the long run and often dangerous in the short of it. But companies whose leadership places God and family before work and encourages their employees to go home at 5:30 or 6:00 create an environment where the most talented people want to continue to work and make their significant contributions. Think about this: Hobby Lobby stores have among the highest employee satisfaction ratings and the lowest turnover rates in their industry, owner David Green is on the 2004 Forbes list of billionaires, and the stores continue to have

> The bad choices of our 20's, 30's, and 40's often must be paid for in the 50's.

a policy of being closed on Sunday to give their employees time off to worship. Just a coincidence? We don't think so.

So many of the high stress numbers we see are due to a woeful imbalance between God, family, and work. This is especially true for single fathers as well as working mothers who are learning that "Super-Mom" is just a myth. It can be done for a while but not for long. Just 13 years ago the average woman in America outlived the average man by 7.1 years. That number is now reduced to 5.4 years. And it is not because men are living longer.

We believe that the Round Table is a great first step. However, it is only one step toward a healthier workplace. Many other initiatives can be taken to improve the workplace environment, for sure. But the Round Table proves to us that executives who play on the same team, and work hard to help rather than compete with each other can create an emotionally healthy organization. Those bright stars of tomorrow are learning today how to ask the critical questions about workplace values, ethics, and business practices regarding the well-being of employees before they bring their talents to the company.

The Stress Test produces an enormous amount of discussion. So one of the most difficult things for the moderators is to know how to control the process. For example, he or she needs to have a sense of when to stop the flow of discussion for breaks and food. Lunch, by the way, should be no more than 30 minutes and the moderators must be responsible for fairly strict timing and the inevitable herding of cats to get everyone back to the circle and away from the cell phones and Blackberries. It is important for the moderators to understand that some of the content of the stress discussion is so engrossing that it is easy to forget that people need breaks and food.

Furthermore, we recommend that the No Zinger Rule only be in effect when the group is in the circle. Breaks and lunch allow "open season" for those executives whose compelling senses of humor must be accorded some venting. This recommendation, of course, is at the discretion of each Round Table.

Most of these pointers may be seen in Chapter 13, "The Secrets Of A Successful Round Table." We offer it because we believe that our simple but effective strategy will change the way executives think and act, especially toward each other.

During our work in the Round Tables, we have observed remarkable and systemic behavior change. We wish we could tell you all or even some of the stories we have witnessed with our own senses. But our Rule of Confidentiality binds us to take these moving, stunning, and sometimes just emotionally overwhelming experiences to our graves.

We can speak in generalities about the process, of course, and that is what we have attempted to do here. But there is no substitute for your own experience and we urge you, (quoting T. S. Eliot again) "Do not ask what is it; Let us go and make our visit."

The Round Table format is so healthy and healing because, when properly moderated, it provides an emotionally safe zone for open, honest, and sincere communication at very deep levels. It allows someone who is suffering to ask for and receive assistance. It gives one person at a time the floor to be heard, without the kind of argument or interruption that can be seen on political talk shows—the very antithesis of the Round Table model.

Healthy companies, like healthy families, create venues for the open, honest, and safe exchange of meaningful, thoughtful dialogue. They create a place where viewpoints can be fully expressed without the fear of censure or rude interruption. These companies and families value listening as much as speaking, for often our most creative ideas come from the thoughtful evaluation of the ideas of others. In order to effectively evaluate them, we must first hear them.

"I don't know what you're talking about with my spouse in there, but whatever you are doing, keep it up. It's working!"

The Round Table is a powerful venue for creative inquiry. It is a think tank at its finest. One of the healthiest aspects of the rules of the Round Table is that they give the group explicit permission to be creative about some of the most bedeviling human problems. In essence, the rules slow down the communication in the Round Table so that the focus is on understanding the problem rather than quickly and efficiently dispatching it so we can get onto the next one.

The Round Table Journey teaches acute listening skills to executives. We know this because we have heard from their spouses. They tell us, "I don't know what you are talking about in there, and I know I can't know, but whatever you are doing, keep doing it because my husband is just a better listener now. He recognizes my need for him to listen rather than to fix."

We have felt for a long time that many executives spend much of their professional time listening to people-problems, anyway. The Round Table gives them specific training in hearing, evaluating, and understanding people-problems that they may or may not have had in college. Our Round Tables often have the feel of the best parts of college (without the beer!) and this adds to the bonding experience.

In effect, the Round Table gives us permission to be each other's teachers and students at a much deeper level than college typically afforded most of us. And just as well. For now the stakes are higher and the game is not just better grades; the game here is life and, as Shakespeare so wisely observed in *Henry V*, "the game's afoot."

Some companies with which we have worked have discovered that the Round Table can be adapted to a variety of business activities. Here are just a few that can be effectively Round Tabled:

- Corporate decisions at the highest level
- Integrating new acquisitions or facilitating mergers
- Conflict resolution between large executive egos
- The emotionally dangerous challenges of family-owned and family-run businesses

The Round Table skills exported out of the sessions also improve all other business meetings. Because Round Table executives have developed genuine empathy and sensitivity to each other's points of view. Their other meetings become more focused and productive, with significantly less energy bleeding off on time wasters such as hidden agendas and posturing. And the result is translated to the bottom line. Our members have reported unanimously that their other business meetings immediately improved as a result of their own growth through the Round Tables.

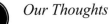

Our Thoughts

❖ The Stress Test is a good clinical measure of the degree of suffering among the Round Table members.

❖ The power of the Round Table model can be used to improve a variety of business activities.

Your Thoughts

1. What is your current stress level? Are you happy with that number? If not, what specific things can you do to change it?

2. Be creative: What areas of your current business or home life could benefit from the Round Table Journey?

ELEVEN

Where Do We Go From Here?

Cheer your heart.
Be you not troubled with the time, which drives
O'er your content these strong necessities;
But let determin'd things to destiny
Hold unbewail'd their way.

Antony and Cleopatra, Act III, Scene IV

After each Round Table, and especially after the first one in which everyone has had the opportunity to tell his or her story and listen to the reaction of the group, we usually end the day with one or two sentences from everyone. These statements answer a simple question:

What happened here today?

The answers are typically varied but they fall into certain major categories. The first one is amazement: "I can't believe that I have been working so long with so many people in this room and knew so little about your lives."

This is often followed by regret: "I am sorry that I did not take the time earlier to get to know so many of you on a deeper level. This has been a very rich and emotionally rewarding day."

This is followed by gratitude: "I am deeply moved that this company cares enough about me as an individual to give me such an opportunity and such a remarkable gift."

This statement in turn is often followed by hope: "I've learned something here today. I discovered that I have made judgments about people in this room without knowing the history behind what I have been seeing. I want to continue to get to know you all better and I hope that you want to know more about me."

Then comes insight: "I am just blown away at how many of us have experienced similar situations without knowing it. We could have been helping each other all along."

Insight is inevitably followed by powerful acceptance: "I know one thing for sure. I feel closer today to everyone in this room than I ever have."

"We could have been helping each other all along."

Then, of course, comes the inevitable good humor: "When I saw the questionnaire for today and heard that we were going to spend the day with the shrinks, I thought, 'Oh God, we're all going to hug each other and sing *Kum-bay-ah*!'"

For the record, we are not offended by the term "shrink." Two of the three of us are named *Zink*, and when you do the work we do, the sobriquet *Shrink* seems inescapable. Besides, we all get tremendous satisfaction at seeing the group shrink closer together. It was the American poet Robert Frost who wrote that he was not frightened by the stars but the spaces in between them.

Knowing that other people are suffering as well does not necessarily ease our pain; but knowing that they have suffered or are suffering in situations similar to our own helps us see that it is not just ourselves who have been singled out for a particularly hard time in life. Laughing (or crying) with others who have been through the same pain cycle in life's washing machine can be emotionally reassuring on many (and often profound) levels.

For one thing, we can learn the awful truth of Shakespeare's observation, *"Sweet are the uses of adversity."* We grow as we hear others who have faced our same troubles answer the question, "What did you learn from this time in your life?" We all experience these things at different times along our life lines. Many of us were told to "keep your trouble to yourself; no one wants to hear it anyway," or "keep a stiff upper lip; just tough it out; don't be such a baby!" As a result, we often "lead lives of quiet desperation" as Henry David Thoreau so famously said.

We hear many different emotions expressed at the end of our Round Table day, but despair has yet to be one of them.

We hear many different emotions expressed at the end of our Round Table day, but despair has yet to be one of them. A lot of people *talk* about team building. From our experience, *talks* about team building are often quite useless. In order for teams to get the feeling that the individuals on the team are actually *on the team*, something must happen to them all that gets them to think and feel like a unit with a single purpose.

Being accepted as part of something greater than ourselves is just plain healthy. Sharing our ideas with someone who cares about them reduces stress. Being there for others as they share their own ideas reduces stress. Having others with whom to share the work load reduces stress. Having someone "watch your back" and knowing we can count on that someone when trouble comes reduces stress. Being needed and appreciated reduces stress. Getting caught doing something *right* reduces stress. Seeing the efforts of others meld with our own efforts to produce common goals and rewards turns stress into *eustress*. One person "in the zone" is rewarding to see; a team "in the zone" creates realities and opportunities for many people that otherwise could not happen. A team in the zone is just plain fun.

Round Tables do not teach about team work. They *are* team work.

In short, working smarter together and not harder alone greatly reduces stress.

We would not be telling the truth here if we said that everyone in our Round Tables appreciates these insights at the end of the first session. But, on some level, a large number do. Round Tables do not teach about team work. They *are* team work.

Why is this different from traditional "group therapy" and why should businesses invest in giving up a day a month or every six weeks to do such a thing? The profit savvy mind says, "What? Tie up my top executives, *all at the same time*, for a day to sit around and listen to each other's pain? Are you crazy?"

Well, it is different from traditional group therapy in this way: In our typical group, *most of the people are healthy.* In fact, when most of the people in our Round Table are *unhealthy*, our success is often minimized. This is so because the unhealthy individuals (depressives; alcoholics; drug abusers; narcissistic, sociopathic, or other aberrant personalities) typically lack the necessary empathic skills to bond or even identify with the other individuals in the group.

Research into group dynamics shows repeatedly that individuals whose thought and/or feeling patterns revolve solely around themselves and who have serious trouble empathizing with others *need individual psychotherapy* before they are sufficiently skillful to contribute in a positive way to the well-being of the group.

Without the Round Table experience, high performance teams can be sabotaged by just one unhealthy member. But they can continue to function because the healthy members develop adaptive and compensatory (co-dependent) behaviors for interacting with the unhealthy member. But if a team has a number of unhealthy members, the healthy ones are overwhelmed by the destructive antics. The stress that everyone feels ultimately destroys the effectiveness of the team.

However, within the Round Table Journey, an unhealthy individual may act like a grain of sand in an oyster: A group of healthy individuals sitting and listening to an unhealthy individual is an education in group dynamics in itself. When the healthy individuals are empowered to speak their minds and share their true observations about what they just heard, it isn't very long before someone says something like this: "You know, Mike, I don't know how you feel about it, but when I went through a very similar period like the one you just described, I sat down with a therapist. Fortunately my pastor, who is also a therapist, was able to recommend this terrific man to help me. I liked this man. I trusted this man. And after a few sessions I got a very powerful feeling that this man was going to really help me. And he did. I was raised to believe that only sick people have to go see shrinks, but that was foolish and short-sighted thinking. That man really made a difference in my life."

A group of mostly healthy people will know when someone in the group isn't behaving in a healthy way. None of the members may have any training or experience in psychotherapy, but the wisdom of the group will find a way to suggest individual help and counseling.

Our Round Tables, of course, have an advantage here since J. has been a practicing psychotherapist for more than 32 years and Tom and Jeffrey have professional counseling experiences totaling more than 40 years. But we are very confident in the wisdom of a group of healthy executives. Often in our own sessions, and before any one of us has raised the issue of private counseling, one of the members will have brought the subject to the forefront.

One thought shows up often: "Where do we go from here? How can we keep this energy flowing?" It is at this point that we usually observe that the group has the power to do whatever it wishes. However, we do offer some suggestions:

First, as we mentioned earlier, meet once a month for at least the first six months, to deepen the bonds that have just been formed. As an aid, we suggest some exercises and questions that will get the ball rolling for each session (see Chapter 14). Secondly, since all members of a Round Table work together in the same company, we recommend that they talk to each other on a regular basis outside the sessions—and much deeper than Level I communication (while still maintaining the confidentiality rule). This will reinforce the empathetic connections. In addition, we suggest members use this connection time to "catch 'em being good," supporting and helping each other with ongoing problems and solutions, all of course without violating Round Table confidentiality. Keep in mind that outside the session any member can share what he or she has said inside the session, and that any member can ask for and receive help from another member. Finally, we encourage everyone to look for ways to use the rules of the Round Table in other aspects of business, for instance, in ordinary meetings. One of our members reports that his division has instituted a "no-zinger" rule at all times—and the results have been remarkably positive: The swords and shields have largely disappeared.

The Round Table is amazingly effective at conflict resolution. Perhaps the most rewarding aspect of this work has been watching members who have had conflict with each other in the past come to human terms with that conflict. Listening to two powerful executives acknowledge to the group that they have had trouble with each other in the past and now realize that they had "made stuff up" about each other can be a great moment in the life of a company. It certainly is a great moment in the lives of these two individuals.

Moments like these give us the sweet balm of hope. It is this hope for a better, healthy life for ourselves, our families, and our colleagues that powers the Round Table Journey.

Our Thoughts

❖ Round Table members are comforted by discovering the value of *not going it alone.*

❖ A group of cohesive, healthy individuals has the power to help a suffering member find a path to healing.

Your Thoughts

3. Have you been in therapy? If so, was it a positive, effective experience? Why or why not? What could *you* have done to make it even more effective?

4. What steps would you take to find an effective therapist for yourself or someone close to you?

Part III: Moderating It

TWELVE

All Things in Moderation

Be cheerful, sir,
Our revels are now ended. These our actors,
As I foretold you, were all spirits, and
Are melted into air, into thin air;
And, like the baseless fabric of this vision,
The cloud-capp'd towers, the gorgeous palaces,
The solemn temples, the great globe itself,
Yea, all which it inherit, shall dissolve
And, like this insubstantial pageant faded,
Leave not a rack behind. We are such stuff
As dreams are made on, and our little life
Is rounded with a sleep.

The Tempest, Act IV, Scene I

Over the years of facilitating Round Tables, we have discovered a set of skills that are essential to successfully moderating the experience. As you have read in the preceding pages, the Round Table is a cauldron of powerful emotions elevated, often for the first time, to the conscious level. In the hands of a moderation team unaware of or unprepared for the forces at work, the results can be nothing short of disastrous. Fortunately, most of the skills required for successful moderation—the ability to insert and remove the control rods of emotional nuclear fission—are neither complicated nor beyond the reach of ordinarily sensitive human beings. While you don't need to have mastered all of these skills, the more you acquire, the more effective you will be. And many of these skills you will master in the process of moderating Round Tables.

A Taxonomy of Skill Sets
for Round Table Moderators

1. A measured, steady tone of voice that creates a feeling of authenticity and trust, especially when introducing the rules of the Round Table.

2. A basic understanding of how stress affects the human body and the ability to communicate this knowledge in everyday language.

3. A basic conceptual framework for the various ego states that comprise the fundamentals of transactional analysis.

4. The ability to listen to one person and monitor the group at the same time.

5. The ability to suspend judgment and evaluation in order to further understand the problem.

6. The skill to engage and draw into participation a person who is not participating.

7. The ability to monitor time during the meeting and the ability to read body language for cues regarding a) lack of interest; b) disagreement; c) distraction; and d) the need for a break.

8. The ability to monitor the room for human comfort issues like proper temperature, lighting and glare, adequate water and soft drinks, name tags, and comfortable chairs.

9. The ability to ask questions for clarification and understanding without sounding either prosecutorial or authoritative.

10. The ability to encourage someone who is emotional to take the time necessary to get his or her thoughts and feelings out before the group.

11. The ability to feel comfortable while someone is getting emotional.

12. The ability to diffuse conflict by encouraging all points of view on a given subject.

13. The ability to remain calm and not defensive when challenged with criticism of the procedure or process.

14. The ability to interact effectively with your fellow moderators.

15. The personal security to operate without an agenda other than the general health of the group.

16. The ability to recognize, draw out, and celebrate dissenting points of view.

17. A sensitivity to group members from cultures other than the predominant culture of the group.

18. The ability to examine an issue from the point of view of someone who is the opposite gender.

19. A general comfort with quiet, which a group sometimes needs to think and process.

20. The ability to introduce new members to an existing Round Table by (a) making them feel welcome; (b) at the appropriate time giving them the opportunity to share some of their personal history; and (c) meeting with them at a break to make sure they are comfortable and feeling part of the group.

21. The ability to explain to the group the departure of a member and to allow the group the freedom to verbally reflect on the loss.

22. An articulated respect for *feeling* as well as *thinking* minds.

23. The ability to "catch 'em being good" by feeling comfortable while sincerely offering words of encouragement and praise spoken directly to someone in front of others.

24. The skill and sensitivity to effectively and sincerely apologize when you have erred.

25. The willingness to learn and grow personally from your experience as a moderator.

26. Follow-up skills between sessions to include calling people you said you would call, getting materials to people who need them, and staying connected with the group for individual work as necessary.

27. The ability and confidence to ask for help.

28. A sense of humor.

THIRTEEN

Secrets of a Successful Round Table

Here are a few administrative and logistics tips to ensure success in setting up the Round Table Journey:

- Limit the number of participants to twelve (not counting the moderators). This ensures that all participants have an unhurried opportunity to share their stories. Consider slightly more, but only with strong justification.

- If this is an initial Round Table, make sure all participants receive the homework assignment (Chapter 15) in a timely manner.

- Find a quiet, isolated room. We strongly recommend going off-site to create a retreat atmosphere, but in any case the location must be isolated from interruption.

- Arrange for very comfortable, boardroom-type chairs to be set up in a circle, with no central table.

- Make sure boxes of tissues are available.

- Make personal contact with the site manager to coordinate the day's logistics, including no interruptions during session, food, temperature, lighting, outside noise, etc.

- Arrange for a continental breakfast to be available beginning at 7:30 a.m.

- The session will begin promptly at 8:00. Ensure participants know that arriving late is a bad choice. It will run until all have had an opportunity to speak. (A conservative estimate is 20-35 minutes per participant, but don't place time constraints when it comes to sharing one's soul.) Everyone should plan to stay until the end (typically 5:00 p.m. or so). Leaving early breaks the atmosphere in the room.

- Arrange for lunch (sandwich buffet is fine) to be available at noon, preferably in a separate room to allow the staff to set it up without interrupting the session. Lunch should last no longer than 30 minutes.

- Arrange for a mid-afternoon healthy snack.

- Ideally, moderators need to share their own stories, but this can be sacrificed when time is an issue.

FOURTEEN

Suggested Exercises

As you have seen, the Round Table format is a wonderful venue for introspection and group bonding. Used properly, it will yield many amazing and unexpected results. Furthermore, we treat the experience as one in which we deal with what emerges. However, we appreciate that some moderators may be nervous about "Where do I go from here?" To help with that anxiety, here are some exercises you, as moderator, might plan to use for your meetings. But do so with caution: The group may need to go somewhere you don't expect. And that's okay.

Introductions:

"Tell us one thing about your professional life and one thing about your personal life that the group does not know. Include as many details as possible so we can get to know you better as a person."

While this exercise may seem self-explanatory, it is important for the moderator to listen carefully to all the details that the speaker provides. These details are often clues to the emotion behind the story. Stories seemingly chosen at random are not always at random and will contain many important clues as to the personality of the speaker.

Many speakers will reveal insights into their own character, worldview, personal history, emotional traumas, and other life-shaping forces that will explain to the group a great deal about why the speaker behaves the way he or she does.

It is important for the moderators to give the group opportunities to ask further questions or make observations about the speaker's presentation after the story has been told. Also, a very effective question to ask the speaker is, "As you were telling us this story about your life were you learning anything about yourself as you heard yourself relate your experiences?"

If a speaker begins to cry as he or she is sharing, it is more than okay. It is important to remember that crying is a good thing. We cry to release tremendous energy which, if held inside us, can do physical and emotional damage to us.

A person who is embarrassed and greatly uncomfortable for crying in front of the group should be encouraged gently and given verbal and non-verbal emotional support. Statements like, "It's okay to cry here, Dave, that is one of the reasons we are here. We are here for you. We all have a powerful need to cry." And, "I admire your courage to show your feelings. You honor us with your tears." (Remember to include tissue boxes in your preparation checklist.)

The group members take their cues from the moderators. If you are excessively uncomfortable, they will be, too. The people in the group will rise to almost any occasion if they are given a chance to do so. Do not tell anyone or the group how to feel; rather let them feel. This experience alone can powerfully move a team from I to WE.

The Stress Test:

"If we could represent your unhealthy stress number on a scale of one to ten, with ten being the worst stress you have ever experienced and one being little or no stress at all, what is your number right now? Also, tell us whether that number is rising, falling, or holding steady. And tell us why."

It is important for the moderators to remember that the stress number is a relative number and not an absolute. The stories *behind* the stress number are the most important part of this exercise, because the group will probably identify with these. After a few speakers share their stories, the commonalities of these stories will begin to bond the group emotionally as they all begin to realize that others in the group typically are suffering with similar or more egregious problems.

Give Me Your Childhood:

"Think back to the long ago days of your childhood or teenage years and tell us a story from your life that best illustrates the person you are today."

These stories are important for two reasons. In the first place, they will give the group what often are stunning insights into the way the speaker views himself or herself in the world today. The second reason is that each story will suggest a powerful self-discovery path for the members of the group to follow as each begins to examine the lives they are living.

Often times, this exercise will surface memories that have lain dormant for decades. It is deeply introspective for the speaker and very illuminating for the rest of the group. Since the introductory request can take some people by surprise (remember, no agendas or e-mail tip-offs about what the day will cover), be prepared, as moderator, to start the group off with a story from your own childhood.

Remember Freud wrote that "there are no accidents." The stories that are told will often suggest to the group what the speaker views as his or her life's mission. As the group comes to terms with the reality that the happiest and most fully integrated people in the group are those *who know their own life mission*, those who are struggling with this challenge will get important clues for further introspection and investigation.

Once again, it is imperative that members of the group have sufficient opportunities to ask questions and share their own reflections after the speaker has completed the task. Be prepared for some wonderful "ah-ha" moments.

This is an excellent time for members of the group to get to observe and comment on the strengths, talents, and abilities of what they know of the speaker and how these flow from the story they just heard.

Color Code:

"Based on your reading of Taylor Hartman's book, what color are you? How does your color help or hinder your interaction with others?"

This exercise is adapted from the work of Dr. Taylor Hartman as documented in his book, *The Color Code*. The exercise is best done after all members of the group have read this insightful treatment of human personality theory.

Hartman maintains that one way of viewing the personality puzzle is through the lens of human motivation. He holds that most of us can be better understood by knowing the principal motivator at our very core. He sees these as basically four:

- Red: Power and achievement;
- Blue: Intimacy and realtionship;
- White: Peace and tranquility; and
- Yellow: Fun.

Hartman does an excellent job of showing how we are born with one color at our core but to survive life challenges successfully, we must learn the healthy skills of the other colors.

The book contains a remarkably succinct test that will teach the student his or her color. Be prepared for great laughter and a very good time. Knowing a person's core color (motivation) can dramatically improve our understanding, trust and level of communication. This exercise takes a full day, but it is well worth it.

Best Boss/Worst Boss:

"Tell us about either your best boss or your worst. Give us as many details as you can remember in one story that will capture this person for us for all time. Please include in your story how this person affected your emotional and/or physical health and that of your co-workers."

This exercise is valuable from two perspectives of leadership. First, it serves as an instructive real world lesson to illustrate the research that says that bosses are the number one reason why people either stay or leave a job. Two, the stories will correlate leadership issues with health issues and help the group reflect on the stories that are told and might be told *about them* someday.

Again, the commonalities of the stories and their collective experience serve as a bonding agent for the group. Almost all American industries are micro-universes in themselves; often people in the group have worked with each other elsewhere and will verify each other's perceptions regarding certain past bosses. This "legacy" effect brings groups to powerful discussions regarding the essentials of leadership. Moderators serve the health of the individuals and the organization by drawing out the skill sets or lack thereof and, in effect, creating a clinic on leadership issues. It is discussions like these that actually constitute leadership skills training in a specific company environment. Studies repeatedly show that one of the most prevalent anxieties among executives is the fear that they will be "found out;" that is to say, their direct reports will believe that they do not know what they are doing.

The bonding through sharing and storytelling actually becomes a strong method for diffusing these anxieties by demonstrating how frequently they inhabit executive mindsets and how ultimately destructive they can be.

The Parent Trap:

"Tell us of your most difficult time as a parent, step-parent, or significant adult in a child's life. Include as many details as you are comfortable giving us. Please

include how you see the roles of parent and business leader as either similar or dissimilar."

This exercise, like several of the others, is designed to focus the discussion on personal stress in the lives of the members. Raising kids, while trying to be effective and successful on the job, is hard and deeply stressful work. This is especially true for men in your group who are single dads and for women in your group who are trying to live the myth of "Super-Mom." And make no mistake: *It is a myth.*

In addition, The Parent Trap is a cross-over exercise, challenging participants to draw parallels and contrasts between the skills required for successful parenting and those required for successful leadership in the business world.

One word of caution here: Avoid the tendency to make this an academic discussion straight out of an industrial/organizational psychology class. Keep it on the personal level by focusing on experiences and *feelings* of the Round Table members. As a general rule, if you feel the discussion is drifting too far into academia, ask the feeling question: "How does that make you feel?"

Childhood's End:

"Some of you may have had experience with caring for your elderly parents. The average woman in America today spends 17 years raising children and 18 years caring for elderly parents. Can you share with us your experiences with this problem?"

This is another exercise whose purpose is to bring out the painful and stressful issues lurking below the surface in the lives of almost everyone in the room. Virtually all participants have dealt or are currently dealing with the gut-wrenching choices of helping aging parents. Be sure to ask for as many details as possible from those who volunteer to speak, since it will become obvious that many people in the room will share in or greatly benefit by the experience. If, for instance, a member volunteers to disclose the heartache of dealing with a mother suffering from Alzheimer's Disease, chances are excellent that someone else in the room has valuable experiential stories to share about coping with the disease. Remember that the purpose is not to tell the member what should or should not be done, but rather to share stories from which one can draw new insights into the present problem.

The detailed sharing will also evoke the frustration, the guilt, the impact on marriages, the accompanying work problems, and some of the medical issues involved—information that can prove deeply valuable to those who have yet to walk through that particular corridor of hell.

As with all other exercises, sensitivity to the speaker and those who respond is key. This is deeply personal pain, and it must be treated with the respect and dignity it deserves.

Mid-Life Crisis:

"Many of you have heard the term 'mid-life crisis,' and as it turns out, this means different things for different folks. If you had had your own version of mid-life crisis, could

you share what happened to you and your family during this painful time in your life?"

The mid-life passage, whether precipitated by some deeply emotional event (often for men, it is the death of a father) or just brought on by other pressures in life, can result in profound changes in the way an individual perceives the world. While in the throes of the crisis, many report that they do not understand it, or recognize the common symptoms. Even afterward, it is often a topic of shame or guilt, and often is accompanied by a feeling of alone-ness—that no one else has ever suffered through the mid-life passage.

But many have survived or by-passed the worst symptoms, and sharing the experience can be a great comfort to those in the group who are making the passage.

Since some of what is shared is deeply personal, this exercise should only be attempted after several effective sessions where the group has become noticeably closer. For what is shared will be a good measure of trust that has developed among the members of the Round Table.

Free-Fire Zone:

"Almost everyone has had the experience of being fired. Please share with the group your own termination story. What were you feeling at the time? What are you feeling now about the event? How do you explain the difference?"

Even those who have not (yet) been fired will gain valuable insight into the process of personal growth in the wake of termination trauma. And in addition to the more obvious stories about "This was the greatest day of my life," you will also see object lessons in leadership begin to emerge. For out of the stories will come specific leadership issues and examples, including the emotional pain that leaders themselves suffer when they must terminate an employee. The lessons shared will provide insight into the best methods for carrying out this inevitable and challenging leadership task.

Emotional Show & Tell:

"Who has something you would like to share with the group today? What is going on in your life that we can help you come to terms with? How can we help you?"

This exercise may sound trivial, but it can produce some powerful results. Used after several sessions of deep connection, this question is a large net to cast into the waters of the Round Table. You may be awed at the catch. A word of caution: Be ready to deal with what emerges. Because it will.

These exercises are merely a few of the many ways to prime the pump and get deep discussion flowing in the group. But we challenge you to engage your creative right brain to develop insightful and sensitive questions of your own. Remember only this: Your primary goal—always— is to help the members reduce individual stress in their lives and to help the group grow closer together and more interdependent. If they do that, you will have surely succeeded in *Helping People Heal*.

FIFTEEN

Round Table Pre-Work

These introspective questions (not meant to be shared with the group) help members prepare for their first Round Table Journey.

Who Are You?

1. What have been the most satisfying moments of your life? Why were they so satisfying?

2. What character traits do you admire most in other people?

3. How do you measure the success of other people?

4. How do you measure your own success?

5. What makes you angry? What frustrates you?

6. Name four or five things that are most important to you.

7. How would the people around you describe your character?

8. How would you like the people around you to ultimately describe your character?

9. Why do you work for your company?

10. What would make you leave the company?

11. What would make you stay?

12. What do you want people to think of when your company comes to mind? Why?

SIXTEEN

Suggested Resources

There are many sources of information out there—some good, some marginal—to help you work on relieving stress and building community, the twin objectives of the Round Table Journey. Here are some of our favorites:

<u>Reading Material:</u>

- *His Needs, Her Needs: Building an Affair-Proof Marriage* - Willard F. Harley, Jr., Ph.D.
- *What Happy People Know* - Dan Baker, Ph.D.
- *The Color Code* - Taylor Hartman, Ph.D.
- *Upbringing* - J. Zink, Ph.D.
- *Motivating Kids* - J. Zink, Ph.D.
- *Dearly Beloved* – J. Zink, Ph.D.
- *Hammer-Proof* - Jeffrey Zink, Ph.D.
- *Choices* - Jeffrey Zink, Ph.D.
- *Eitel Time* – Charlie Eitel, Ph.D.
- "Leading by Feel" – *Harvard Business Review*, January 2004

<u>Web References:</u>

www.zinkuniversity.com
www.jzink.com
www.jazink.com